Contents

What is nuclear power?   4

The world's energy needs   6

Fossil fuels   8

Nuclear energy   10

Background radiation   12

Nuclear power stations   14

Nuclear safety fears   16

Dealing with waste   18

High-level waste   20

Further research   22

Nuclear fusion   24

Public concerns   26

The future of nuclear waste   28

Further information   30

Glossary   31

Index   32

Words printed in *italics* are explained in the glossary.

What is nuclear power?

Nuclear power is an industry that has developed over the last 50 years to create large amounts of electrical *energy* that can light cities. However, as well as producing energy, nuclear power stations also produce waste, and it is this waste that causes *environmental* concern.

It takes a huge amount of energy to light up a city like New York.

Sellafield nuclear power station in Cumbria, UK.

Why do we need nuclear power?

Electricity is mainly *generated* using coal and oil (also called *fossil fuels*), but demand is growing faster than these fuels can supply. Nuclear power can generate enormous amounts of energy without using fossil fuels. Some countries, such as France and Japan, do not have natural sources of fossil fuels and, instead of buying in oil and coal from other countries, they prefer to rely upon nuclear power.

Because nuclear waste is so dangerous, people have to wear special protective suits when working with it. The suits must cover them completely.

What's wrong with nuclear power?

The major problem with nuclear power is its waste. The material left over after electricity has been made is extremely dangerous to all life. It is *radioactive* and severely damages living *cells* that are exposed to it. Plants wither and die; animals and people can develop cancers and die.

Dealing with nuclear waste

No one has yet found a way to make nuclear waste totally safe. So far the waste we have is buried or covered so heavily in concrete that we hope its effects are controlled. Scientists are continuing to work on how waste can be treated more effectively.

Burning fossil fuels releases clouds of potentially harmful gases into the atmosphere.

Fifty years from now

Today, the United States and Europe use most of the electrical power in the world. However, China and India's demands for electricity are growing rapidly. It is thought that in 50 years' time the world's electrical needs will have more than doubled. If fossil fuels create this electrical energy, *global warming* could have disastrous effects on world *climate* (see pages 8–9). And if nuclear power is used, large quantities of highly harmful waste material will need storing. We need to find solutions fast.

The world's energy needs

A modern kitchen contains many appliances that run on electricity, such as kettles, cookers, microwaves and fridges.

Different types of energy are used to move, stay warm, listen to the radio, or light a room. As world populations rise, more energy is needed to make sure that people can travel and live in relative comfort.

How much fuel do we use?

One way to see how much energy we use is to look at oil. In 1999, the world used about 20,160,000,000 litres of oil! And this is just oil, we also use coal and natural *gas*, as well as nuclear energy and others.

In many less developed countries, such as Bangladesh, food is cooked over a fire.

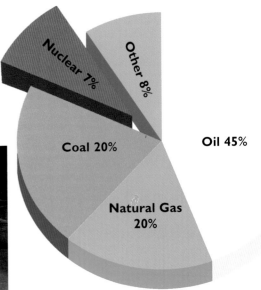

Nuclear 7%

Other 8%

Coal 20%

Oil 45%

Natural Gas 20%

The percentages of fuels used in the world in 2000.

How much energy do you use?

If you have a washing machine, dishwasher, oven, fridge, stereo, television and toaster in your kitchen, you will use the equivalent of just over 420 litres of oil a year to keep them working. And that's just the kitchen.

Dishwasher
92 litres

Oven
84 litres

Fridge
128 litres

Washing Machine
100 litres

TV
22 litres

Toaster
5 litres

Stereo
7 litres

◆ How you can help

Think about the ways you can save energy. Here are some ideas:
• turn off lights when you leave the room
• don't leave TVs and computers on when you are not using them
• ask your parents to turn down central heating and air conditioning
• take public transport or walk – don't use cars if you don't have to
• find out about your school – are lights and heating turned off when the building is empty? Suggest to your head teacher that the school monitors how much energy it is using.

The growing need for energy

In 1999, the USA, with a population of 284,620,000, consumed 25% of all the energy used in the world. Compare this to countries with outstandingly large populations such as China (1,328,006,000) who used 8% and India (1,027,015,000) 3%. Scientists have *forecast* that over the next 20 years the greatest expansion of fuel usage will be in the developing world, especially Asia and South America. They predict that by 2020 global energy use will have risen by 59%, most of this in Asia.

Another interesting statistic is that each person in the USA uses twice as much energy as people living in most of Europe and about 10 times as much energy as people in China.

Crops today are harvested with machinery that uses large amounts of energy from fossil fuels.

Fossil fuels

Fossil fuels are found in the ground in the form of oil, coal and gas. They have developed over millions of years. We discovered how useful they could be as sources of energy during the 19th century. However, using fossil fuels has two major drawbacks: they release gases that pollute the atmosphere, and the supply may run out.

Oil and coal

Oil and coal resources have formed over the last 350 million years from dead plant and animal life. They have been found all over the world. Today, oil and coal are mainly used for transport – all our cars, trains and aeroplanes run on oil of one sort or another – and for generating electricity in power stations.

Oil rigs like this one retrieve oil from deep under the sea bed.

Coal-fired power stations release gases that may harm our atmosphere.

Natural gas

Experts believe that greater use of natural gas will reduce the amount of *carbon dioxide emitted*, or released, into the air compared to burning coal and oil. Many new power stations are now gas-fired.

These trees have been damaged by acid rain – a result of burning fossil fuels.

Waste products

Burning oil and coal to release their energy also releases the gases carbon monoxide and carbon dioxide into the air. Carbon dioxide is now thought to cause climate change by acting with the Sun to warm up our atmosphere. This is known as the *greenhouse effect*. Other elements released include sulphur and nitrogen. These combine with the water vapour in the atmosphere to form acids which damage both animal and plant life – this is acid rain.

Are supplies running out?

It is not easy to work out how much oil, coal and gas is still available. It is generally thought that we will have enough coal for a few more centuries, but oil and gas will be in short supply in only a few decades. This means that all the fossil fuels that have developed over millions of years will have been completely used up in just a few hundred years. So alternative energy sources, such as nuclear power, are needed.

◆ Science in action

Testing the greenhouse effect

You will need: 2 glass bowls, a piece of glass, 2 thermometers

Place a thermometer in each bowl and stand both bowls in the sun. Carefully place the piece of glass over one bowl. After an hour check the temperature in both bowls. Which one is hotter? The glass cover acts like the greenhouse gases in our atmosphere. It traps the heat from the Sun, raising the air temperature in the bowl in the same way as the gases trap heat, raising the temperature of the environment.

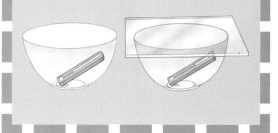

Nuclear energy

Nuclear energy gets its name from the central part of an *atom* – the *nucleus*. Everything in the world is made up of different types of atom. An element is something that is made of only one type of atom.

electrons circling around the nucleus

nucleus containing protons and neutrons

What is an atom?

Atoms are made up of three different *particles*: neutrons, protons and electrons. The nucleus contains protons and neutrons, and the electrons circle around the nucleus. The numbers of each of these particles differ for every element. Hydrogen is the smallest atom – it has just one electron and one proton. *Uranium* is a large atom – it has 92 electrons, 92 protons and 143 neutrons. Most elements are stable – their atoms always keep the same balance of these particles. However, some elements are unstable. Their atoms continually change by emitting some of these particles. These elements are radioactive.

Radioactive elements

When an atom changes, it releases energy. In radioactive elements, the energy is released in the form of heat, light and *radiation*. Radiation can be rays or particles of matter. It happens in a number of ways:

Alpha particles

An alpha particle is a combination of neutrons and protons emitted by the nucleus. This radiation does not travel far and is stopped by most solid objects.

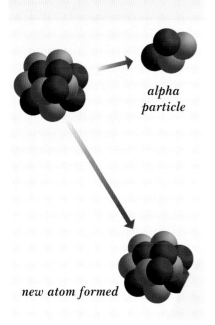

alpha particle

new atom formed

Beta particles

A beta particle is an electron sent out by the nucleus. This radiation travels a few metres and can go through our bodies, but is stopped by metals.

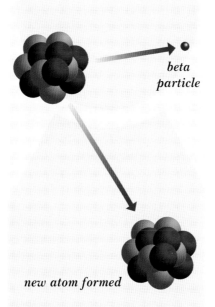

beta particle

new atom formed

Gamma rays

Sometimes the nucleus emits a wave of energy, which is called gamma radiation. These waves travel several kilometres, but can be stopped by lead or thick concrete.

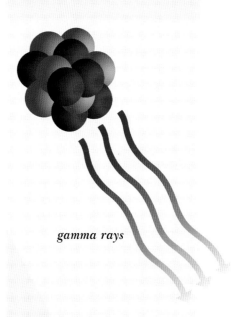

gamma rays

Neutrons

Sometimes the nucleus breaks down emitting streams of neutrons. These travel even farther than gamma rays, but can be stopped by anything containing hydrogen, for example, water.

Half-life

To understand more about how we use radiation, it is important to know about half-life. The half-life is the time it takes a radioactive element to lose the first half of its radiation. The second half of the radioactive decay can take millions of years. For example, Carbon 14 is a radioactive atom with a half-life of 5700 years. If you start with 100 atoms of Carbon 14, after 5700 years you would have half of them left (50). After another 5700 years you would have just 25 atoms left, and so on.

Background radiation

Radiation is the release of energy as waves or particles. It can take the form of light and sound, as well as radioactive rays. It is a natural part of the universe. People come across radiation as part of their everyday lives from a variety of sources. This radiation is called 'background radiation'.

Radiation from the Sun

An Austrian scientist, Victor Franz Hess, discovered in the 1930s that the Earth is continually bombarded with radiation from the Sun and other stars. He found out that radiation levels increased the further you got from the Earth's surface. People travelling in an aeroplane are more affected by radiation than those on the ground.

Granite rocks such as these often contain radioactive material.

Radiation from the Earth

Some rocks contain radioactive materials and these affect the soil and water around them. The rocks most likely to contain radioactive material are granite and other volcanic rocks. Although most background radiation is harmless, these rocks can sometimes release the gas radon, which is very dangerous to life.

A lot of background radiation comes from the Sun.

Many homes have smoke detectors. These contain radioactive material.

Man-made radiation

Some of the radiation we encounter every day comes from our own use of radioactive materials. If you have an X-ray you are exposed to radiation. Smoke detectors use a tiny amount of a radioactive substance. None of this is really harmful. The effects of the nuclear industry have also released radiation into our atmosphere. Nuclear explosions and leaks from nuclear power stations have contributed about 0.6% of the background radiation found in the atmosphere.

◆ Science in action

Invisible forces

You will need: a bar magnet, a piece of paper, iron filings (ask your science teacher for these)

Sprinkle the iron filings on to the piece of paper. Now lift the paper over a bar magnet and look at what happens to the iron filings. You have just detected a magnetic force, which is invisible to the eye, just as radiation is.

Geiger counters are used to measure radioactivity.

Measuring radioactivity

A scientist called Hans Geiger invented a device that is used to measure radioactive levels. The Geiger counter is designed to make a clicking noise when it gets near radioactive material. The more clicks heard the higher the level of radiation.

Nuclear power stations

Over the last 50 years scientists have developed ways of using the energy released from the atom to create an energy industry. Nuclear power stations today supply around 20% of the world's electrical energy, and in some countries, such as France, it helps to generate around 75% of the electrical energy needed.

Nuclear reactors

A *nuclear reactor* creates electrical energy to be used in our homes and workplaces. It does this by using the energy released when an atom's nucleus is 'split'. This process is called *nuclear fission*.

This power plant in Brokdorf, Germany, runs on nuclear power.

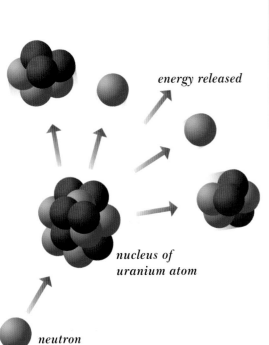

energy released

nucleus of uranium atom

neutron

Nuclear fission

The atoms of radioactive elements can be split into two smaller pieces. The element with the easiest nucleus to split is uranium. The large uranium atom is unstable and releases neutrons. These neutrons bump into other uranium atoms and cause them to split, and this then becomes a *chain reaction*. A tremendous amount of energy is released from such a chain reaction. Nuclear power stations are built in such a way that this energy can be released safely. If the reaction is uncontrolled you get a nuclear explosion.

Power stations

The uranium used in a nuclear power station is contained in fuel rods. These are surrounded by *control rods*, *coolant fluid* and a concrete shield. The control rods make sure that the chain reaction doesn't happen too fast. Nuclear fission produces a lot of energy in the form of heat. The coolant fluid takes this heat away from the reactor core and uses it to heat water to create steam. The steam powers a *generator* that produces electricity.

Built for safety

For safety, the rods and fluid are all contained within a steel vessel especially designed to withstand very high temperatures. The whole reactor is enclosed in a concrete building, which is designed to stop the gamma radiation escaping.

When the fuel rods have to be changed, the workers use machines to handle them.

Science in action

You will need: test tube, sand, stop watch, thermometer

Put a small amount of sand in the test tube and measure its temperature. With your thumb over the end, shake the test tube vigorously for two minutes. Now measure the sand's temperature again. Has it changed? Why?

This shows how movement energy (shaking) can become heat energy, in the same way as the movement energy of the nuclear chain reaction becomes heat energy.

Working in a nuclear power station

All workers are checked for radioactivity.

The people who work in a nuclear power station have to make sure that they are never exposed to radioactive material. They wear protective clothing and handle radioactive material from a distance, using mechanical arms behind glass partitions. The workers themselves are regularly checked for radioactivity to make sure that they have not been affected.

Just as generators using fossil fuels create products that are unwanted, so do nuclear power stations. Most of the waste from a nuclear power station is radioactive.

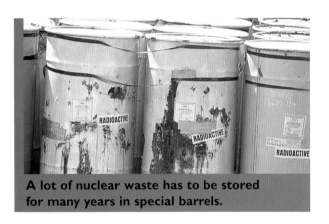

A lot of nuclear waste has to be stored for many years in special barrels.

This sign warns that there is something radioactive behind this fence.

Never safe

All the fuels used by nuclear power stations, such as uranium and plutonium, continue to release radiation even after they have been used – sometimes for billions of years. Some of these fuels will never be really safe.

Radiation sickness

A large dose of radiation will kill a large number of cells, creating an effect similar to being badly burnt. Radiation also affects cell division, the process by which tissues reproduce themselves or grow. The damage can lead to cancer.

These children's illnesses were caused by radiation from a nuclear plant explosion.

This stream has been affected by radioactive pollution.

Public concerns

People living near a nuclear power station are very concerned that their environment might be affected by radiation through leaks, either into the water system or into the land. They fear the possibility of a nuclear 'meltdown', where the reactor explodes releasing radiation into the atmosphere. And because all power stations create waste, people are concerned that the waste is dealt with safely. The nuclear industry is obviously aware of all these fears, and campaigns to tell people how carefully it monitors the environment around its sites. The industry is spending millions of pounds on research to develop more effective ways of dealing with waste.

Decommissioning

The most significant waste in the nuclear industry is the power station itself. When a power station comes to the end of its useful life it needs to be shut down. The process of shutting down a nuclear power station is called decommissioning. The reactor building is the most awkward to shut down because it still contains radioactive material. The only solution the industry has come up with is to cover the whole building with thick layers of concrete to contain the radioactivity.

◆ Sustainable solution

There are a lot of natural sources of energy – the wind, flowing water, the Sun, the sea, hot springs (geysers). All of these are being used today to help us generate electricity. Enormous turbines are turned by the wind, dams use the force of rushing water, solar panels (right) pick up energy from the Sun and wave-power systems use the sea's waves to make electricity. These sources of energy are never-ending and non-polluting. They are called renewable energy sources.

Dealing with wast

The objects and equipment used in nuclear power stations can be affected by radioactivity. Even the workers' clothing is treated as nuclear waste – it is considered contaminated, or made dangerous, by radiation.

National waste policies

There are no international agreements on how to deal with any form of nuclear waste. Some countries do not even have a national policy for dealing with waste. Outlined on the next few pages is a summary of what is generally done. However, there are no guarantees that all countries with nuclear power deal with their waste responsibly.

Very low-level waste may be dumped in ordinary landfill sites.

Low-level waste

Those articles that have had minimal contact with radioactive materials are called low-level waste. This includes waste rock from uranium mines, the clothing from scientists working with radioactive materials, and material used in hospitals for X-rays and so on. Usually very low-level waste is dumped with other non-radioactive waste in sites which are then covered with a layer of soil. This covering is enough of a barrier to the radiation.

Ocean dumping

Some low-level waste is sealed in steel drums and dumped in the ocean. In Britain sea dumping in the Atlantic was the main form of waste disposal until 1983, when the policy was ended.

Barrels of nuclear waste are sometimes dumped in the sea.

Concrete is used to prevent any radioactive leaks.

Intermediate waste

The next level of waste, called intermediate, cannot be dealt with so simply. This material is much more radioactive than low-level waste and needs to be disposed of with more care. Usually intermediate waste is encased in steel and concrete and stored near the power station that created it.

These steel drums of nuclear waste have been covered in concrete before being buried.

Burial

The latest planning on how to deal with intermediate waste is to bury it. The site has to be carefully constructed to ensure complete safety that will last for many years, as intermediate waste will remain radioactive for hundreds of years. The steel drums containing the waste are covered in concrete then buried in a pit lined with more concrete. Above the pit another layer of concrete is constructed as a further safety precaution.

High-level waste

Every so often the fuel rods in a reactor need replacing as the radioactive material completes its half-life. These fuel rods are high-level waste. The decommissioning of nuclear weapons also produces high-level waste as the warheads are taken apart and the most dangerous parts need to be safely stored. The main concern about this waste is that it will remain harmful for over a hundred thousand years.

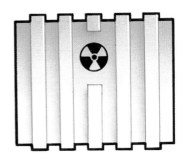

Amount of high-level waste

Power stations produce only a small amount of high-level waste every year. In size it would be equivalent to a small car. However, even this small amount can do immense damage and it needs to be stored safely.

Water pools

One type of radiation, neutron radiation, does not pass through water, so some power stations keep their high-level waste not just in steel and concrete but also in water pools. The plan was that these water pools would only be a temporary storage place until the material could be dealt with elsewhere. However, some waste has now been in water pools for 20 years and space in these pools is running out. Plans for its proper disposal need to be made as soon as possible.

Used fuel rods from nuclear power stations are very high-level waste.

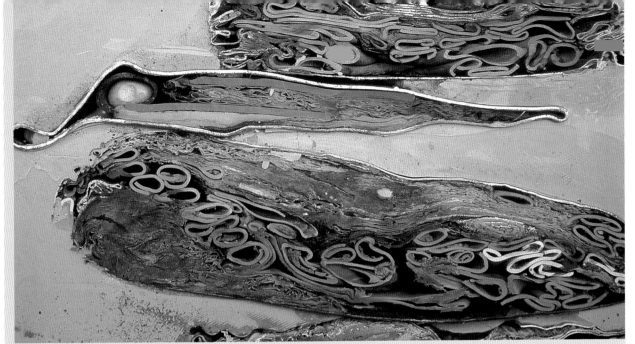

This nuclear waste has been covered in glass and cement for storage.

Burial

The nuclear industry plans to encase high-level waste in glass, which does not decay, and then bury it in deep mines. The mines have to be kept open so that if, in the future, scientists discover a way to make the waste safe, it can be brought back to the surface and treated.

Yucca Mountain mine.

◆ Science in action

You will need: 2 apples, 2 pieces of paper, 2 plastic bags

Take one apple, one piece of paper and one plastic bag and place them on the window sill. Bury the other set in some soil. After a week, record what has happened to each item both in and out of the soil.

Different objects take different amounts of time to decay. Some objects will not decay at all unless treated in some way (such as the plastic bag). All waste needs to be disposed of thoughtfully so that we don't end up creating mountains of rubbish that never disappear.

Concerns with burial

Because the waste remains dangerous for such a long time, the areas chosen for the mines must be extremely stable. There should be no earthquakes, the level of water in the ground should not rise to meet the waste and there should be very few people living nearby. Such sites are not easy to find. In the USA, scientists picked a site in Yucca mountain, Nevada, for deep mine burial. However, it is thought that this area is prone to earthquakes and the mountain range used to be volcanic. Scientists are trying to predict whether or not there will be a volcanic eruption in the next hundred thousand years.

Further research

Because there is no safe way to dispose of high-level nuclear waste, the nuclear power industry is raising billions of pounds to research possible answers to long-term disposal.

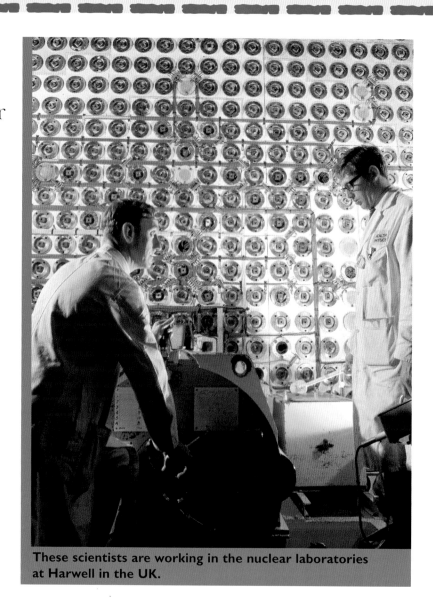

These scientists are working in the nuclear laboratories at Harwell in the UK.

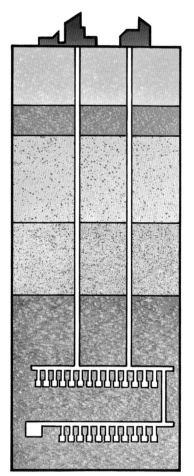

One possible solution is to dispose of nuclear waste in holes deep underground.

Other disposal methods

In the short term nuclear scientists have been working on safer methods of disposal. One of the suggestions is to pour radioactive material into very deep holes in the ground. The material should be so hot that it melts the rock. The rock and material then mix and cool. So far it is not clear how much radioactivity would escape from such a method. Another suggestion is to place waste in holes drilled in the ocean floor. However, if radiation leaked it could seriously damage the marine life.

Efficient use of nuclear fuel

It is possible for a nuclear reactor to make more fuel than it uses. These reactors are called breeder reactors and they have been developed to make fuel last 50 times longer than fuel in standard nuclear processors.

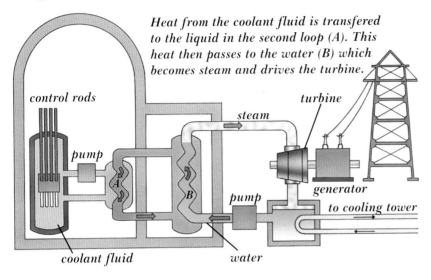

Heat from the coolant fluid is transfered to the liquid in the second loop (A). This heat then passes to the water (B) which becomes steam and drives the turbine.

Scientific solutions

The ultimate solution would be to convert radioactive material to a stable substance. The nuclear industry is funding scientists to study this. More research needs to be done on whether or not we can speed up atomic change, and therefore the release of radiation, so that the radioactive material will become harmless. There is another possibility that involves using a different form of nuclear reaction – *nuclear fusion* (see pages 24–25).

Spent fuel rods are reprocessed at this plant in Sellafield, Cumbria, UK.

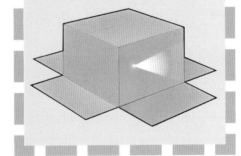
Reprocessing

Nuclear scientists have developed methods for changing the spent fuel rods back into useable fuel – this is called reprocessing. The theory is that instead of having to find storage places for spent fuel rods, the industry can reuse the same fuel and therefore not have to store it. The advantages of this process are that less uranium is dug from the ground and there is less waste to store.

Nuclear fusion

Our nuclear reactors work by nuclear fission. This means that atoms are split to release energy. However there is another way in which atoms change, called nuclear fusion, when atoms combine. Fusion releases huge amounts of energy.

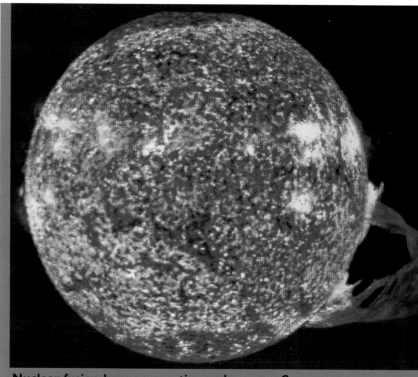

Nuclear fusion happens continuously on our Sun and on all the other stars of the universe.

two different types of hydrogen nuclei fuse together

helium nucleus

energy released

electron

The Sun

Nuclear fusion is the most common form of nuclear reaction in the universe. The main element on a star is hydrogen, which fuses with another hydrogen atom to become helium. It happens when there is immense pressure (gravity) and it releases enormous amounts of heat. This causes the star's temperature to rise to over 10 million degrees Celsius. This is called a thermonuclear reaction.

Recreating fusion

It may seem impossible but scientists are working on ways to recreate nuclear fusion in the laboratory. They are keen to do this because nuclear fusion uses hydrogen, an element we have in great supply (water is made from hydrogen and oxygen). We would not need to mine fossil fuels and we would not have to deal with radioactive materials.

Pollution-free energy

The other major benefit is that nuclear fusion does not create any radioactive waste. Fusion is also unlike fission in that it does not run out of control and cause a massive explosion. As far as scientists can predict there would be no harmful waste at all.

Seas and lakes are great sources of the hydrogen needed for nuclear fusion.

The problems

The main problem scientists face when trying to recreate nuclear fusion is that it needs exceptional pressure and temperature. The latest theory is that we may be able to use lasers to help recreate the conditions that are found in the stars. However, it is generally thought that it is only a matter of time before we work out how to achieve nuclear fusion, which would mean that the reactors of today are just stepping stones in the direction of unlimited fuel and pollution-free energy.

Lasers are currently used to help scientists study the stars. In the future they may be used to recreate the conditions found there.

Public concerns

Environmental organisations, such as Greenpeace, campaign to make the public aware of the dangers of nuclear power and its waste. As a result people are concerned about living near power stations, near waste disposal sites and along the routes where nuclear waste is transported.

Environmental organisations such as Greenpeace campaign for public safety.

The container being unloaded from this ship in France contains spent nuclear fuel.

Transportation

Within the US, throughout Europe and even further afield, nuclear fuel and waste is transported from power stations to storage sites. This transportation has generated a huge amount of public anger, particularly as there have been some accidental leaks of radiation along the way.

Nuclear protests

In Germany, the government planned to develop a waste storage site in Gorleben, Lower Saxony. However, people strongly objected to this, and protesters sabotaged the railway lines. In March 1997, 30,000 police in full riot gear were needed to protect the first shipment of nuclear waste from Bavaria to Gorleben. This cost more than £40 million.

Siting disputes

In the USA, in 1994 Minnesota state allowed Northern States Power (NSP) to store containers of spent fuel at its Prairie Island power plant in Goodhue County. NSP was allowed to do this on the condition that they found a permanent alternative site. So far every site that has been selected has been turned down by pressure groups. And the Mdewakanton Sioux Community who live on Prairie Island desperately wants the fuel removed. There is still no solution to this situation, and NSP have nearly filled their storage area.

The simulator room at Prairie Island nuclear power station.

Public pressure

People can put pressure on governments to act responsibly regarding their nuclear policies. This can have dramatic effects on government policy regarding nuclear energy. For example, in the USA no nuclear power stations have been built since 1978. In Germany, the new government of 1998 reversed its country's nuclear policy and is committed to closing down its 19 nuclear power stations over the next 10 to 20 years. However, is this really the answer?

Police are spraying these anti-nuclear protestors with water in order to stop them blocking this railway line in Germany.

The future of nuclear power

The energy industries are in a very difficult position – they need to create enough energy to meet people's demands, while at the same time producing that energy with acceptable levels of waste.

Scientists predict that the demand for energy in Asian countries such as China will increase hugely in the next 20 years.

Fossil fuels versus nuclear

Scientists largely agree that the waste gases from fossil fuels create acid rain and smog as well as contributing to global warming. The countries of the world have joined together to discuss these concerns and to try to reach an agreement on how much fuel they should be using. The agreement is called the Kyoto Protocol after the Japanese city where the conference took place. Unfortunately not every country could agree to the terms, most notably the USA, which means that the US government does not have to force its citizens to use energy more efficiently or to use less fossil fuel. Nuclear power does not contribute to greenhouse gases at all and therefore some countries see it as a good environmental alternative.

Climate conference in Kyoto, Japan, 1997.

Constant source of fuel

Because the nuclear industry does not need huge quantities of fuel, unlike the fossil fuel industry, there is no fear that the minerals used will run out. With the new technologies of reprocessing and breeder reactors, the fuel can be made to last even longer.

The fuel inside these rods can be reused if it is reprocessed.

Until scientists find ways to make nuclear waste safe, barrels of nuclear waste will continue to be stored underground.

Research on safety

It is in the interests of the nuclear industry to find solutions to their waste problems as quickly as possible. Nuclear scientists receive huge amounts of funding in the hope that they can solve these problems. They are also trying to discover how we might reproduce nuclear fusion, the 'pollution-free' process of energy production. The hope is that in the next 50 years we will have achieved both these goals.

Further information

There are websites where you can find out more about topics mentioned in this book.

www.radwaste.org

www.bnfl.com
The British Nuclear Fuel site incorporates a section called the Learning Zone especially for children with information as well as games.

www.nei.org/scienceclub/index.html
Children's information on nuclear energy with animated cartoons.

www.cleanerand greener.org/
Ideas and help on how to live a greener and more energy-efficient life.

www.edisonkids.com/
Fun games to do with electrical energy.

www.academyofenergy.org
Gaining awareness of energy and our uses of it.

www.energy.gov/kidz/kidzone.html
United States Department of Energy's Kids Zone with lots of activities and fun.

www.globalwarming.com
An environmental protection group dedicated to saving the Earth's natural resources and ending environmental pollution.

www.greenpeace.org/~nuclear/
Greenpeace's views on the nuclear issues of today. For more information about the organisation's environmental campaigns in Australia, check out **www.greenpeace.org.au**.

www.ea.gov.au
The Environment Australia website offers up-to-date information on the latest environmental research and initiatives. There are pages on many different topics including the greenhouse effect and pollution.

Glossary

Atom

The smallest part of a substance that can take part in a chemical reaction.

Carbon dioxide

One of the gases that are given off when fossil fuels are burnt.

Cells

The smallest parts of a living being that can exist on their own. Human bodies are made up of millions of cells.

Chain reaction

A rapid series of events in which each event causes the next one. In a nuclear reactor the chain reaction is the continuous splitting of atoms.

Climate

The weather conditions that occur over a particular area.

Coolant fluid

Liquid that carries heat from the nuclear reactor to the steam generator.

Control rods

Rods that are used to speed up or slow down the chain reaction in a nuclear reactor.

Emit

To send out or release.

Energy

The power to do work.

Environment

The natural surroundings of an animal or plant.

Forecast

To predict what might happen in the future.

Fossil fuels

Coal, oil or gas used to produce energy.

Gas

A substance neither solid nor liquid, for example oxygen and hydrogen.

Generate

To produce something.

Generator

A machine that changes mechanical energy into electrical energy.

Global warming

The heating of the Earth's atmosphere caused by the greenhouse effect.

Greenhouse effect

The way in which certain gases in the Earth's atmosphere trap heat rather than allowing it to escape out of our atmosphere. Carbon dioxide is one of those gases.

Nuclear fission

When a nucleus is split. This releases large amounts of energy and is used in nuclear reactors.

Nuclear fusion

When the nuclei of two atoms combine together to form one heavier nucleus. This reaction produces a huge amount of energy. Nuclear fusion happens continuously in the Sun.

Nuclear reactor

The device which generates electrical energy by splitting atoms.

Nucleus

The core of an atom.

Particles

Tiny specks of matter.

Radiation

The energy given out in invisible rays by atoms during nuclear fission.

Radioactivity

The breakdown of the nucleus in an atom which gives off radiation.

Uranium

The metal used in nuclear reactors.

Index

acid rain 9, 28
alternative energy 9, 17
appliances 6, 7
atom 10, 11, 14, 24, 31

background radiation 12–13
burial 19, 21

cancer 5, 16
carbon dioxide 8, 9, 31
chain reaction 14, 15, 31
climate 5, 9, 31
concrete 5, 15, 17, 19
control rods 15, 23, 31
coolant fluid 15, 23, 31

decommissioning 17, 20

electricity 4, 5, 6, 8, 14, 15
elements 9, 10, 11, 14, 24
energy 4, 5, 6, 7, 10, 11, 12,
. . . . .14, 15, 25, 28, 31
environment 5, 9, 17, 26, 28, 31

fossil fuels . 4, 5, 6, 7, 8–9, 16, 28, 29, 31
fuel rods 15, 20, 23, 29
fuel supplies 8, 9

Geiger counter 13
global warming 5, 28, 31
greenhouse effect 9, 31

half-life 11

Kyoto Protocol 28

natural gas 6, 8, 9
nuclear fission 14, 15, 31
nuclear fusion 23, 24–25, 29, 31
nuclear power 4–5, 6, 9, 14, 15,
. . . . .24, 25, 26, 28–29
nuclear waste 4, 5, 17, 18–23,
. . . . .25, 26, 27, 29
nucleus 10, 11, 14, 24, 31

ocean dumping 18
oil .6, 7, 8, 9

pollution 8, 17, 25
power stations 4, 8, 13, 14–15, 16,
. . . . .17, 18, 20, 27
public concern 17, 26–27

radiation 11, 12–13, 15, 16, 17,
. . . . 18, 20, 22, 23, 31
radioactivity . . .5, 10, 11, 12, 13, 14, 15,
. . . . 16, 17, 18, 19, 20, 22, 23, 31
reactor . . . 14, 15, 16, 17, 23, 25, 31
renewable energy 17
reprocessing 23, 29
research 5, 22, 23, 25, 29

safety 5, 15, 16, 19, 29

uranium 10, 14, 15, 16, 18, 23, 31

workers 15